The Story of

Mary

Mary was a special person and her parents were very special too! Their names were Joachim and Anne.

Mary grew up in Israel, in a little town called Nazareth.

One day, when she was a teenager, something very special happened! She was visited by a messenger from God – Gabriel the Archangel.

"Blessed are you among women," Gabriel said. "You will give birth to God's Son!"

"I will do as God tells me," Mary replied.

Mary was very quick to say "yes" to God.

Mary went to visit her cousin Elizabeth who was also expecting a child. When Elizabeth saw Mary, she was filled with the Holy Spirit and said, "You are the mother of my Lord!"

Mary rejoiced and said, "The Lord has done great things! From now on all generations will call me blessed."

God provided a special man to care for
Mary and His Son. His name was Joseph and
he was a carpenter.

Mary and Joseph were very humble and took care of Jesus.

Jesus loved His mother very much!

When Jesus became a man and began His special work, Mary sometimes accompanied Him.

Even when others abandoned Jesus, Mary
stood next to Him at the cross.

When Jesus saw His mother and His devoted apostle John with her He said, "Woman, behold your son." Then He turned to John and said, "Behold your mother."

Jesus made sure His mother was taken care of.

Jesus suffered for our sins. Mary suffered in her heart at the sacrifice of her Son.

After Jesus rose from the dead, He told His followers to wait for the promise of the Holy Spirit. The Holy Spirit was sent to them from Heaven on the day of Pentecost.

Jesus loves Mary, and we do too!